Text: Alice Fisher
Jacket/Interior Design: Kimberly Adis
Interior Layout: Kimberly Shake
Photographer: Alexandra Grablewski
Executive Editor, Series: Shawna Mullen
Assistant Editor, Series: Timothy Stobierski
Series Art Director: Rosalind Loeb Wanke
Series Production Editor: Lynne Phillips
Copy Editor: Candace B. Levy

The Taunton Press
Inspiration for hands-on living®

The Taunton Press, Inc., 63 South Main Street,
PO Box 5506, Newtown, CT 06470-5506
e-mail: tp@taunton.com

Threads® is a trademark of The Taunton Press, Inc.,
registered in the U.S. Patent and Trademark Office.

The following names/manufacturers appearing in *Beautiful
Burlap* are trademarks: Etsy™, Fray Check™, Jo-Ann Stores℠,
Michaels®, Styrofoam®, Walmart®

Library of Congress Cataloging-in-Publication Data in progress
ISBN 978-1-62710-988-8

Printed in the United States of America
10 9 8 7 6 5 4 3 2 1

contents

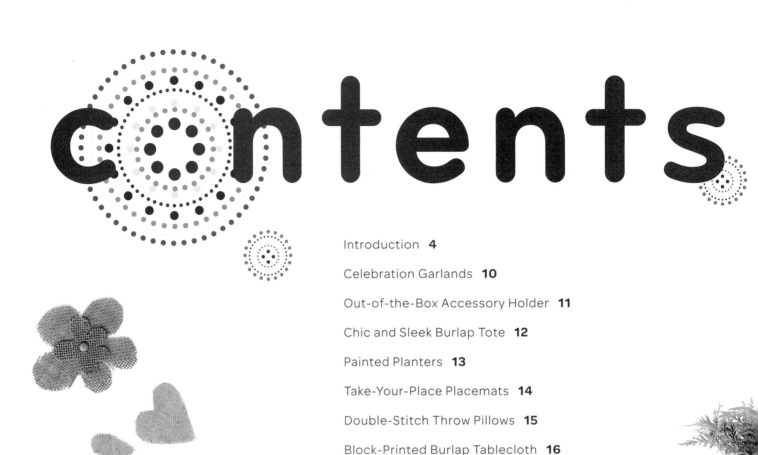

Introduction **4**

Celebration Garlands **10**

Out-of-the-Box Accessory Holder **11**

Chic and Sleek Burlap Tote **12**

Painted Planters **13**

Take-Your-Place Placemats **14**

Double-Stitch Throw Pillows **15**

Block-Printed Burlap Tablecloth **16**

Place-Setting Pockets **17**

Travel Tic-Tac-Toe Game **18**

Herb Garden Flags **19**

Grain Sack Planter Pouch **20**

Blooming Burlap Wreath **21**

Shabby Chic Ruffled Lamp **22**

Happy Holidays Gift Bags **23**

Line-It-Up Table Runner **24**

Rustic Nature Candle Votives **25**

Very Vintage Boutonnieres **26**

Burlap Button Baubles **27**

Lovely Lavender Sachets **28**

Home Sweet Home Address Pillow **29**

Contributors **30**

Resources **31**

introduction

What's the first thing you think of when someone says the word *burlap*? Potato sack races? Gardening supplies? Maybe your cousin's scarecrow costume from 1982? Burlap, also known as Hessian cloth, has come a long way and has quickly become a material that crafters of all types flock to. Despite its rough texture and slightly messy cr-aftermath (cutting burlap produces a lot of lint!), it's a very versatile material that yields projects from shabby chic home décor to rustic wedding essentials to clean and modern design accessories.

Woven from the fibers of the jute plant, burlap is really the workhorse cloth of the textile industry. Its primary use was once as a wrap for bales of cotton or hay and as the material for grain sacks to transport wheat, rye, and barley. Now, this biodegradable product is also one of the most fashionable. From barn wedding decorations to home-office bulletin boards, this affordable, humble, and durable fabric is a great choice for craft projects.

Working with Burlap

While you don't need any specialized tools to create master crafts with burlap, there are a few techniques and housekeeping guidelines to keep in mind when working with this material.

There are many variations in the weaves of burlaps, so choose the weave best suited for the project on which you are embarking. Consider the stiffness of the fabric and the openness of the spacing between fibers. For example, if you are making a pillow, you'll want a tighter weave to prevent the stuffing from escaping. If you are making curtains, but you want light to come through, consider a looser weave.

If you love the look of burlap but don't like the feel, you can spend a little more money and purchase linen burlap. It has the same thick, fibrous look, but has more bend and is softer to the touch.

Burlap is a rough material. Try to imagine when you are cutting or sewing through it, that it's treating your tools as if it were sandpaper. If you use your good fabric scissors or sewing machine needles on burlap, you'll notice they'll become dull very quickly. Designate a set of scissors, sewing needles, and utility or rotary blades to your burlap crafts and accept that you'll be changing blades and sharpening scissors more often than you're used to.

tips

SEWING WITH BURLAP

Choose your needle to suit the weight of your burlap. For a heavyweight variety, opt for the 100/16 universal or denim needle. For something a bit thinner like a medium-weight, choose the 80/12. For hand sewing, use a size 5 to size 7 hand-sewing needle. It's best to use a strong cotton, polyester, or cotton/polyester blend thread. As a general rule, when you send burlap through your sewing machine, you want the tension high and the stitches longer. A stitch length of 1.75 mm to 2 mm is recommended. Depending on the project, a zigzag stitch can also a good idea. Make sure to clean your sewing machine after working with burlap. The jute fibers will end up everywhere and you want to make sure that your machine is clean and ready for its next use.

If you are using an open-weave burlap, it's best to back it with muslin or linen if you want your project to appear solid. This extra layer of fabric works as a barrier for any kind of stuffing and acts as a stabilizer for the stitch to grab on to. If you are making something that has two sides of burlap and both need backing because of the open weave (like a pillow or tote bag), stack the cut pieces in this order: muslin, burlap, burlap, then muslin. Sew all four together, and then flip them inside out so the burlap is on the outside. Because burlap tends to unravel, come apart, and fray quicker and easier than most materials, give yourself an extra 1 in. of seam allowance for sewing projects.

If you are using a pattern on an open-weave burlap, instead of cutting out the shape and then sewing, first trace the pattern onto the back of the burlap. Put it through the sewing machine and sew the seam before cutting. This helps prevent the burlap from fraying and coming apart when over-handled. You can also trace the pattern onto the muslin or linen liner, stitch it, and then cut. You'll see that tracing a pattern onto muslin is much easier than tracing onto burlap.

If you anticipate pulling or stress on the seams of your sewn burlap project, go with a tighter weave. Stress and tight stuffing will literally cause the seams of the project to fall apart, and once this happens, it's very difficult to repair.

It's not uncommon to find slubs in your burlap, an accidental irregularity caused by knotting, twisting, or uneven lengths of the fiber. This has a tendency to skew the stitches when it's sewn over. Before you cut out your pattern or plot your design, scan the burlap carefully to make sure any slubs will not run under the stitches.

STORING BURLAP

Burlap is best stored in a dry, cool environment. Since it's a natural material, it likes to draw moisture from the air and can mold easily, in even a slightly humid space. Avoid storing it in direct sunlight. The sun and heat will dry out the burlap, causing it to become brittle. If burlap stays folded for any long period of time, you will see that the creases become pretty stubborn. It's best to roll it around a tube or hang it. If you have to fold it, try to fold it on a crease in the design.

CARING FOR BURLAP

Burlap and washing machines don't mix well together. The agitation moves the fibers rather aggressively and your burlap will lose its shape and possibly fall apart at the edges. It can also cause problems in your machine, as burlap produces an enormous amount of lint.

Hand-wash burlap in a clean sink or bucket with cold water (warm or hot water might shrink the fabric) and a small amount of gentle detergent. Never leave the burlap in the water for longer than 5 minutes, as the water will cause the burlap to come apart and fray. Rinse it well, and then dry it flat between two towels. Avoid twisting or wringing it out.

Blot the burlap with a wet sponge to spot remove any stains. Blot on top of the wet spot with a dry towel immediately.

If you need to get rid of an odor from your burlap, there are a few methods, depending on the severity of the odor. For minor scents, just put it outside in the sun for a few hours. If the sunshine doesn't cure the issue, leave the fabric outside and sprinkle it with baking soda (best for use on smaller pieces of burlap). Let the baking soda sit for a few days, then shake it off. If the scent is stubborn, spray the burlap with a little water mixed with white vinegar or lemon juice. Rinse the burlap with water and let it dry flat between two towels. (Do not combine the baking soda and vinegar solutions, as a chemical reaction can occur.)

techniques

Burlap has a mind of its own, and knowing the best way to work with it will make crafting more enjoyable and less frustrating.

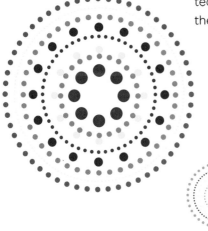

CUTTING A STRAIGHT LINE

Measure to where you want to cut and make a tiny slit into the edge of the burlap (if needed). Grab hold of one fiber/burlap string, and pull it out slowly, pushing the piece of burlap down like you're pulling a drawstring. This will leave a channel and a straight line for you to follow with your scissors in between two fibers. You can also use this technique as a design element (see the table runner on p. 24).

FRINGING

The rough and unfinished edges of burlap add to the natural, effortless quality of it. To create fringe, just grab and pull an outside jute fiber and remove it completely. Always pull only the outermost string; if you try to pull out several strings at one a time, you can create a messy tangle.

To keep the fringe in its place, either sew a zigzag stitch up the length of the unfinished edge to hold the fibers intact, or use a strip of fabric, glue with twine, seam binding, or ribbon to keep the adjacent strings in place. You can also try using a liquid seam sealant like Fray Check™ to hold the fibers together.

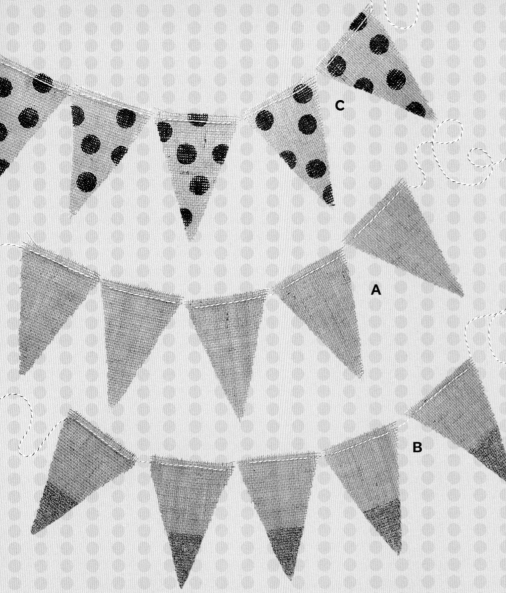

Celebration Garlands

These easy-to-make buntings (**A**) are suitable for birthdays, holidays, or any days!

SKILL LEVEL
Beginner

MATERIALS
Cardstock
Pencil
Ruler

Scissors
Burlap
Parchment paper
Decoupage glue of your choice
Glitter
Sponge brushes
Acrylic paint
Bottle cork
String or twine
Needle
Hole punch (optional)

TO MAKE THE GARLANDS

1. Draw a triangle on the cardstock to create a pennant template that measures about 4 in. wide and 6 in. tall. Use this template to cut as many burlap triangles as you need for your garland.

2. Decorate the triangles, if desired. To make the glittered garland (**B**), lay the triangles on parchment paper and paint the bottom third of each one with the decoupage glue. Sprinkle with glitter and let it dry for about 1 hour. Remove the garland from the parchment paper and shake off the excess glitter. To make the polka-dot garland (**C**), brush paint onto the round end of the cork and then stamp it onto the burlap. Repeat as desired.

3. Use the needle and string to connect the pennants. Simply connect the top corner of one pennant to the next. You want to leave enough string between each pennant so that the garland will drape, (½ in., as shown in the photo). Continue across the garland. If you do not want to use needle and string, you can cut or punch a small hole at each top corner and tie the triangles together with twine.

Out-of-the-Box Accessory Holder

Take your necklaces and bracelets out of the drawer and show off your costume bling on an elegant display board.

SKILL LEVEL
Intermediate

MATERIALS
Cardboard
Scissors
Glue of your choice
Cork sheet
Quilt batting
Stapler
Burlap
1½-in.-wide ribbon
Bronze upholstery tacks

TO MAKE THE ACCESSORY HOLDER

1. Cut 3 pieces of cardboard to 18 in. by 24 in. Place a dab of glue in the corners of one sheet of cardboard and layer the second on top of it. Repeat with the third sheet of cardboard and let dry. Then glue a sheet of cork on top of the stack of cardboard. (You can use cork squares as a substitute.)

2. Tightly wrap 2 layers of batting around the cardboard and cork and staple to the back. Cover the batting with burlap and wrap tautly. Staple the burlap to the back. Lay the ribbon along all four edges, about ¼ in. from the edge, and staple the ends on the back. This will look best if you first place both long sides and then both short sides.

3. Press upholstery tacks evenly spaced around the edge. Use more tacks for hanging the jewelry.

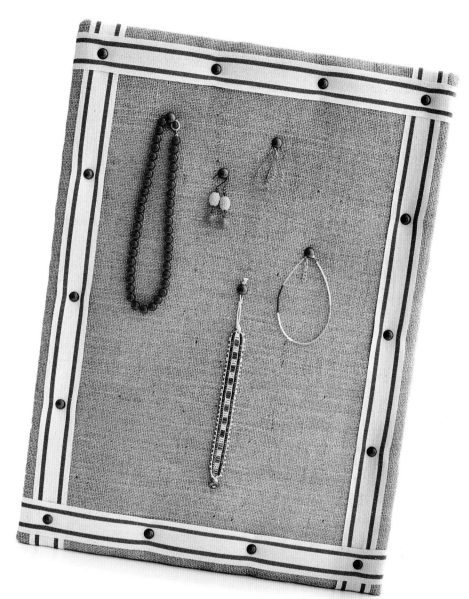

TIP Staple a 4-in. piece of ribbon on the back of the cardboard. This will let you hang the jewelry display wherever you want! Or just lean the board against a wall or on your desk for easy access.

Chic and Sleek Burlap Tote

DESIGNED BY LAUREN KRUKOWSKI

You can carry this stylish bag to the beach, the grocery store, and everywhere in between.

SKILL LEVEL

Intermediate

MATERIALS

Thick white twine

Ruler or measuring tape

Scissors

20-in. by 14-in. by 6-in. burlap tote

Glue of your choice

Black burlap

TO MAKE THE TOTE

1. Cut seven 15-in. and five 21-in. pieces of twine. Divide the face of the burlap tote into a six by four grid with the white twine. (Each square will be approximately 3 in. by 3 in.) Glue the twine to the bag.

2. Cut twenty-four 2½-in. squares of black burlap. Fray each square about ¼ in. on each side.

3. Glue the black squares into the open grid spaces on the burlap bag. Apply glue around each square along the outer edge of the intact fibers. (This will hold the square together and prevent it from fraying further.) In the bottom corners, fold and glue the squares around the bottom corners.

TIP Get creative with your grid! Instead of making squares of all the same size, make them irregular to get a more dynamic look. You can also use different colors to great effect—either use colored burlap or paint the burlap shapes before gluing them in place.

Painted Planters

Rescue soup and coffee cans from the recycling bin and give them a facelift. With burlap's natural attributes, it's the perfect material for pretty planters.

SKILL LEVEL

Beginner

MATERIALS

Cans

Burlap

Scissors

Measuring tape

Painters' tape

Paint

Paintbrushes

Glue of your choice

TO MAKE THE PLANTERS

1. Remove the labels from the cans and make sure the cans are adequately washed and dried. Cut the burlap about 1 in. taller than the can and ½ in. wider than the circumference of the can.

2. Place the burlap on a covered work surface and adhere horizontal stripes of painters' tape, evenly spaced. Paint in between each strip of tape and let it dry.

3. While the paint is drying, cut another burlap band that measures about ½ in. shorter than the can height by the circumference of the can. Glue this piece to the can about ¼ in. from the top edge .

4. Once the painted burlap is dry, glue it on the can on top of the first burlap piece, tucking ½ in. under the bottom and ½ in. around the top edge neatly.

> **TIP** Stripes not your thing? Make polka dots instead! Simply paint a piece of burlap the color of your choice and, once the paint has dried, cut out your dots. You can vary the size of your dots for added interest or try other shapes: stars, hearts, or flowers would be adorable.

Take-Your-Place Placemats

DESIGNED BY LISA LEMIEUR

Vintage-inspired numbered placemats (**A**) add character and flair to any table setting.

SKILL LEVEL

Intermediate

MATERIALS

Burlap
Scissors
Ruler
Sewing machine
Thread
Stencils
Painters' tape
Stencil sponge brush
Acrylic paint

TO MAKE THE PLACEMATS

1. Cut two 14-in. by 18-in. pieces of burlap for each placemat.

2. Layer the two pieces of burlap on top of each other and machine-sew together around the entire perimeter, about ⅝ in. from the edge on all sides. (Doubling up the burlap in this way gives the placemats a more solid weight and feel.)

3. Pull the threads on all four sides at the edges to make a fringe. Tape the stencils to the bottom right corner of the placemat. So the paint doesn't bleed underneath the stencil, dab it on with a stencil sponge brush. Stencil the numbers onto the burlap and let the paint dry.

B

VARIATION

It's easy to make table numbers instead of placemats (**B**)! First, determine how many table numbers you will need and how large you want them. Cut that many sheets of wood to your desired size (I used 8-in. by 9-in. pieces of wood). Wrap your burlap around the blocks of wood and secure it on back with glue. Then stencil on your numbers and let the paint dry.

A

Double-Stitch Throw Pillows

DESIGNED BY LAUREN KRUKOWSKI

Burlap might be the last material you'd think of resting your head on, but the hand-stitched yarn stripes soften the surface of these stylish throw pillows.

SKILL LEVEL
Advanced

MATERIALS
Burlap
Scissors
Linen
Measuring tape
Thick yarn
Yarn needle
Pins
Thread
Sewing machine
Pillow stuffing
Needle

TO MAKE THE PILLOW

1. Cut a piece of burlap to the desired size of your finished pillow, plus 1 in. on each side for seam allowance. Cut a piece of linen to match each burlap piece.

2. Thread the yarn needle with a strand of yarn about 1 in. longer than the length or width of the pillow you are stitching. Hand-stitch the yarn through one piece of burlap following a single thread of burlap from edge to edge to keep it in a straight line. Add more lines of yarn. Alternate the stitch length and the space between lines of stitching for visual interest.

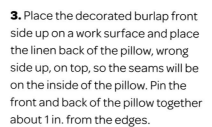

3. Place the decorated burlap front side up on a work surface and place the linen back of the pillow, wrong side up, on top, so the seams will be on the inside of the pillow. Pin the front and back of the pillow together about 1 in. from the edges.

4. Thread the sewing machine and set the tension to 4 and stitch length to 0. Sew three sides of the pillow using a ½-in. seam allowance; then sew again with a ¼-in. seam allowance. The double stitching will help prevent the seams from moving or coming apart.

5. On the fourth side of the pillow, leave a 5-in. opening to stuff the pillow. The opening should be at least 2 in. away from either edge to keep the four corners uniform. Mark the sides of the 5-in opening with

pins. Using the sewing machine, sew from each edge of the pillow to the edge of the opening using a ½-in. seam allowance; repeat using a ¼-in. seam allowance.

6. Remove all of the pins, and turn the pillow right side out. Stuff the pillow. If the stuffing is lumpy, fluff it with your fingers to remove the lumps before putting it in the pillow. Make sure each corner is adequately stuffed (you can use a chopstick to push the stuffing into place, if necessary).

7. Close the opening of the pillow by pinning the burlap and linen together, leaving the seam allowance inside the pillow. Hand-stitch the opening closed using a needle and thread. Use small stitches to hide the seam.

Block-Printed Burlap Tablecloth

Use the visible threads of burlap to help guide your block printing or go wild and stamp outside the lines.

SKILL LEVEL

Beginner

MATERIALS

Scissors

Ruler

Craft foam

Cardboard

Glue of your choice

Acrylic paint

Burlap (large enough to cover your table)

Painters' tape

Paintbrush

Seam sealant of your choice

TO MAKE THE TABLECLOTH

1. To make your stamp, cut a 3-in. by 2-in. triangle from craft foam. Glue the foam triangle to three layers of cardboard to create a stamp.

2. Mix three to five colors of paint. You can use multiple shades of the same color or completely different colors—it's up to you!

3. Starting on the left edge of the burlap, adhere two lines of painters' tape, spaced about 3 in. apart, to the length of the tablecloth to act as a guide for your triangle stamp.

4. Apply paint to the foam triangle and, using the tape to line up the edge of your stamp, stamp triangles down the first column of your tablecloth. You can space them evenly or at irregular intervals to give the design a more abstract look. Once you have completed the first line, move the first strip of tape 3 in. to the right of the second strip and repeat the stamping process.

5. Apply seam sealant to the edges of the tablecloth to keep it from fraying. The burlap will not hold up well in the wash, so spot clean with a damp cloth as necessary.

> **TIP** If you have a child's wooden block on hand, it makes a great shape and form for stamping. Trace the block onto craft foam, cut, and glue it to the block.

Place-Setting Pockets

DESIGNED BY LAUREN KRUKOWSKI

Handy holders to house utensils will not only add style to your table, but will keep your tablescape looking clean and tidy.

SKILL LEVEL

Advanced

MATERIALS

Burlap

Scissors

Measuring tape

Thread

Pins

Iron

Sewing machine

TO MAKE THE POCKETS

1. Cut the burlap into 15-in. by 5¾-in. rectangles. Set the sewing machine tension to 4 and stitch length to 0. Using a ½-in. seam allowance, sew across one short side of the burlap rectangle.

2. Fold the sewn edge of the burlap rectangle up 5 in. to make the pocket. The pocket should measure 5 in. by 5¾ in. Press the fold to make sure the burlap lays flat. Sew across the bottom of the pocket, ¾ in. from the fold.

3. Sew both the left and the right long sides from the bottom fold to the top, using a ½-in. seam allowance and leaving a raw edge. Measure 1⅝ in. in from each side seam and sew from the bottom fold to top edge, creating the three pockets that will each hold a utensil. This will leave you with a 1⅞-in. pocket in the middle.

4. Sew across the top short end of the place-setting pocket, using a ½-in. seam allowance and leaving a raw edge. Repeat to make additional place-setting pockets.

Travel Tic-Tac-Toe Game

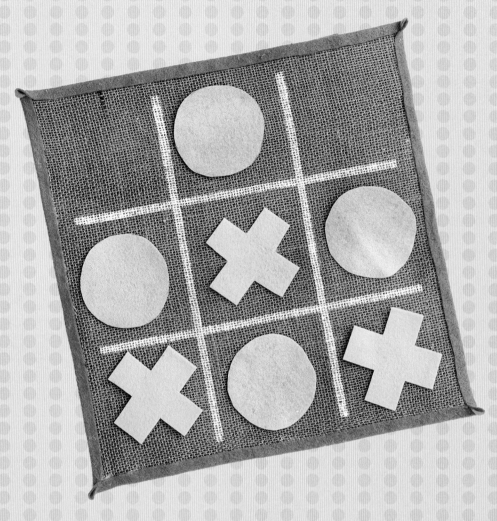

Mix soft and smooth felt with rough and bumpy burlap to make a classic game that's good on the go.

SKILL LEVEL

Intermediate

MATERIALS

Felt (3 colors)

Burlap

Scissors

Fabric glue of your choice

Painters' tape

White acrylic paint

Sponge brush

Ribbon

TO MAKE THE GAME

1. Cut a 13-in. square of felt and a 12-in. square of burlap. Center the burlap square on top of the felt square. Fold the felt edges over the burlap and glue them down. Repeat for all four sides.

2. Pinch the corners together and glue. Paint a tic-tac-toe grid onto the burlap using painters' tape as a guide. Measure in 4 in. from the sides to create the grid lines. Let the paint dry.

3. Cut five 3-in. circles from one color of felt and five 3-in. X's from the remaining color of felt.

4. Use fabric glue to adhere two 12-in. pieces of ribbon, spaced 5 in. apart, to one of the back edges of the board. Roll up the game board with the felt circles and X's inside and tie the ribbons to store.

Herb Garden Flags

Burlap and gardening have a long history together, so it feels only natural to craft plant markers with it.

SKILL LEVEL
Intermediate

MATERIALS
Burlap
Scissors
Ruler
Iron
Large letter stamps
Ink pads
Colored embroidery floss or thin twine
Needle
Thin stick
Garden shears

TO MAKE THE FLAGS

1. Cut a strip of burlap that's 3 in. wide and 8 in. long. (This size works for a four-letter flag with the stamps I used. Judge the size based on the stamps you have.) Fold the burlap in half lengthwise and press to form a nice crease.

2. Ink your stamps generously one at a time and stamp onto the folded strip, with the crease on the right-hand side.

3. Thread the needle with the twine and stitch the top and bottom edges of your flag. You want to use a seam allowance of about ¼ in.

4. Pull two threads of the burlap off the top and bottom edge to get a small fringe. Cut the end of the stick with garden shears to make a sharp point and thread it through the burlap on the open end.

Grain Sack Planter Pouch

DESIGNED BY SHAYNA ORRINO

The handmade logo tag on this delicate hanging pouch references the vintage burlap grain sacks from the early 1900s.

SKILL LEVEL

Intermediate

MATERIALS

Burlap

Scissors

Sewing machine

Thread

Jute twine

Glue of your choice

Linen

Computer

Printer

Iron-on transfer paper

TO MAKE THE POUCH

1. Cut a piece of burlap that's 6 in. by 18 in. and fold it in half lengthwise. Thread the sewing machine and increase the stitch length a bit. Sew each side all the way to the open edge. Snip off the bottom corners on the outside of the stitched edge so it creates a square bottom.

2. Cut a 12-in.-long piece of twine and glue it to the inside of the pouch to serve as a hanger. Once the glue dries, turn the pouch inside-out. Use a pencil to push out the corners.

3. Trim a piece of linen to 3 in. wide by 3½ in. long. Fray the edges by pulling just a few outer threads.

4. Design the logo of your choice on your computer, flip the image in your editing software, and then print it on iron-on transfer paper. Follow the manufacturer's instructions for transferring the image to the linen.

5. Press the burlap pouch flat, then use glue to adhere the tag.

> **TIP** If you don't want to use editing software, you have some options. You can stamp a design directly onto your burlap bag. Or you can stamp the design onto a piece of linen and sew or glue the linen to the bag. If you choose to do this, you'll want to sew the linen to the burlap before you stitch the sides together (to ensure that you don't stitch the label through both layers of the bag).

Blooming Burlap Wreath

Use brightly colored burlap to add a little spring cheer to this classic, floral door décor.

SKILL LEVEL
Beginner

MATERIALS
16-in. Styrofoam® wreath
Burlap ribbon
Straight pins
3 colors of burlap, about ½ yard of each
Scissors
Colored brads
Glue of your choice
Twine

TO MAKE THE WREATH

1. Wrap the burlap ribbon around the wreath, overlapping each wrap slightly to achieve full coverage. Secure in the back with straight pins.

2. Cut daisy-shaped flowers freehand from the colored burlap. Cut various sizes, from 2 in. to 5 in. in diameter. Stack two or three of one color together and fasten in the center with a colored brad.

3. Glue 7 to 9 flowers onto the wreath in a pattern to your liking. Cut a 3-in. piece of twine, knot the two ends together, and glue the knot to the back top of the wreath to create a hanger.

TIP If you love flowers, but aren't a fan of wreaths, feel free to leave the wreaths out of the picture! The flowers make wonderful décor for the walls of a child's room. Just cut the flowers, layer as desired, and tack in place on the wall.

Shabby Chic Ruffled Lamp

DESIGNED BY TERRA SHEPARD

Soften up a plain old lampshade with this textural burlap treatment, perfect for any bedroom sanctuary.

SKILL LEVEL

Intermediate

MATERIALS

Lampshade

Burlap (1½ yards for a shade that is 12 in. tall and 2½ feet in diameter)

Scissors

Glue of your choice

Iron

TO MAKE THE LAMP

1. Cut a piece of burlap about 2 in. taller than the lampshade and ½ in. wider than the circumference of the shade.

2. Position the burlap piece on the lampshade folding over about 1 in. along the top and bottom edges. To prevent seeing any glue leaking through the burlap on the outside, glue the burlap to the shade along the inside top and bottom of the lampshade. Pull the burlap taut as you go.

3. Cut the rest of your burlap into strips. Cut them about 1½ times as long as your shade is tall, and 3 in. wide. Fold the strips in half lengthwise and press with the iron until you get a solidly creased seam.

4. Apply 2 in. to 3 in. of glue along the outside of the crease and glue it onto the shade in a squiggly line. Hold the burlap strip in place until you feel the glue has set. Ruffle each strip differently as you glue to add interest to your design or keep the ruffle consistent for a more elegant look.

5. Once your lampshade is full to your liking, fill in any gaps that look too large or awkward with additional burlap strips.

Happy Holidays Gift Bags

With these sweet drawstring pouches, the gift packaging might be more adorable than what's inside!

SKILL LEVEL
Beginner

MATERIALS
Duct tape
Scissors
5-in. by 7-in. drawstring burlap bags
Freezer paper
Pencil
Iron
Sponge brush
Acrylic paint

TO MAKE THE BAGS

1. Wrap a piece of duct tape around your hand, sticky side out. On the side of the bag on which you are going to apply your stencil, blot the surface of the burlap with the tape to pick off any loose fibers.

2. Draw or trace your template onto the non-shiny side of the freezer paper and cut out the shape so you have a stencil. Place the stencil onto your bag, shiny side down, and use the iron to press into place.

3. Paint inside the stencil and let the paint dry. Remove the stencil carefully. You can use each stencil up to three times before you have to cut a new one.

TIP If you love to play with textures, trace your design onto felt or any other material of your choosing, cut it out, and hand-stitch it in place.

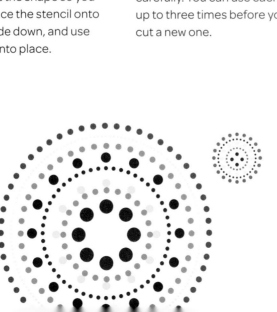

Line-It-Up Table Runner

Embrace the simple construction of burlap and make this minimal striped table topper by creating a design with negative space.

TIP This burlap runner will not hold up well in the wash, so be sure to spot clean as necessary.

TO MAKE THE TABLE RUNNER

1. Cut a piece of burlap 14 in. wide by the length of your tabletop. Fray each long edge until you have ½ in. to ¾ in. of fringe.

2. Working across the short side of the burlap runner, pull a fiber about 2 in. from the edge of the burlap and remove it. Pull about 10 fibers to create a 1-in.-wide stripe.

3. Continue creating stripes by pulling the burlap fibers. Create narrower stripes by pulling fewer strings and thicker stripes by pulling more.

4. To keep the long sides of the runner from fraying over time, glue a piece of thin rope or twine along both edges of the runner.

Rustic Nature Candle Votives

Seashells and acorns combine Mother Nature and a touch of ambiance to create these upcycled baby food–jar votives.

SKILL LEVEL
Beginner

MATERIALS
Baby food jars
Burlap
Scissors
Glue of your choice
Seashells
Acorns
LED tea lights

TO MAKE THE VOTIVE

1. Peel the label off the baby food jar and cut a piece of burlap to that size.

2. Glue the burlap around the jar, securing at the seam.

3. Glue seashells or acorns to the front of the jar and place your candle inside.

> **TIP** Want to create a larger votive? Just cut a piece of burlap to cover a larger jar and follow the directions as given. Get creative with your embellishments! Next time you get a bouquet of flowers, dry them and glue them to the burlap to enjoy the gift even longer. Or cut out some burlap flowers, as described for the "Blooming Burlap Wreath" (p. 21), and glue the clusters on for a permanent floral display.

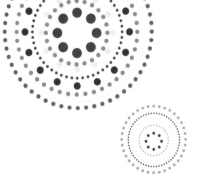

Very Vintage Boutonnieres

DESIGNED BY SUZANNAH STANLEY

These easy-to-craft lapel pins add a handmade touch to a handsome line of groomsmen.

TO MAKE THE BOUTONNIERES

1. Cut 3½-in. by 2½-in. leaf shapes from the cardboard. Cut one for every boutonniere that you need. Glue the brown side of the cardboard leaves to the burlap and let them dry. Trim the burlap to the edge of the cardboard.

2. Cut the skewers to 3¾-in. long by first scoring them with scissors and then breaking them. Make one per boutonniere. Glue one stick to the center of each leaf on the burlap side.

3. To wrap the stem of the boutonniere, glue one end of the twine to the bottom of the stick. Then apply a thin line of glue up the back of the stick 1 in. at a time, wrapping the twine as you go. When you reach the top of the stick, trim the twine to fit, and glue in place to the stick.

4. Glue two feathers where the stick meets the burlap leaf. Cut an 11-in. piece of ribbon, tie it in a bow, and glue it to cover where the stick, feathers, and twine come together.

5. Glue three to four buttons on top of the feathers, just above the bow. Glue a pin back to the back of the cardboard, just behind the bow.

> **TIP** You can go a more classic route by attaching a tiny flower arrangement instead of the feathers and buttons.

Burlap Button Baubles

DESIGNED BY KATHLEEN KRAUS

These are so quick and easy to make, you can craft a different set for every day of the week!

SKILL LEVEL
Beginner

MATERIALS
Cover button kit
Solid cotton fabric to match the burlap
Burlap
Scissors
Earring posts
Bobby pins
Glue of your choice

TO MAKE THE BAUBLES

1. Cut the fabric and burlap into a square that's a little larger than the button.

2. Place the burlap over the rubber button tool and then layer the cotton fabric over it. Press the metal button into the center of the tool.

3. Trim off the excess fabric, leaving some to be pushed into the center of the now-covered button. Push the excess fabric in.

4. Press in the flat part of the button until it clicks. You have now covered a button! Glue your buttons to the earring posts (**A**) or bobby pins (**B**).

> **TIP** If you don't have cotton fabric to match each burlap color, you can paint the metal button a hue to match.

A

B

Lovely Lavender Sachets

The natural material and breathable weave of burlap makes it the perfect material for fragrant drawer sachets.

SKILL LEVEL

Beginner

MATERIALS

Burlap

Ruler

Scissors

Sticky note (3 in. by 3 in.)

Glue of your choice

Dried lavender buds

Twine

Essential lavender oil

TO MAKE THE SACHETS

1. For each sachet, cut two 6-in. squares of burlap. Fringe 1 in. on each side. Place a sticky note in the center of one piece of burlap and apply a line of glue just outside 2 adjacent sides of the paper. Immediately stack the second burlap square on top of it, lining up the edges.

2. Apply another line of glue on the third side of the sticky note, and press to seal. Once the glue is completely dry, remove the sticky note.

3. Fill the pocket with dried lavender buds. Shake the buds down into the pocket then apply another line of glue to seal them in.

4. To hide the glue line on the outside of the sachet, glue a piece of twine on top and tie in a knot in the center of one of the square's sides.

TIP Refresh the scent of the lavender every so often by applying a few drops of essential oil to the sachet.

Home Sweet Home Address Pillow

DESIGNED BY AUTUMN SPEER

This rustic pillow will hold up well against the elements and make it easy for guests to know when they're at the right house!

SKILL LEVEL

Advanced

MATERIALS

Burlap

Muslin

Scissors

Computer

Printer

Tape

Contact paper

Stencil stipple brush

Acrylic paint

Pins

Sewing machine

Thread

Pillow stuffing

Needle

TO MAKE PILLOW

1. Cut two 16-in. by 24-in. burlap pieces and two muslin pieces of the same size.

2. Design your address using the software of your choice. Remember that your pillow will be stuffed and you want to have about 2 in. on either side of the address so it's readable from a distance. Print it out and tape it to a piece of contact paper.

3. Cut out your stencil. Adhere the contact paper stencil to the burlap and use the stipple brush to dab the paint on. Do not brush the paint! It will get under the stencil and you won't have a clean, painted line. Let the paint dry and remove the stencil.

4. Stack the fabric in this order: muslin, burlap, burlap, muslin. Pin around the fabric, about 1 in. from the edge. Thread the sewing machine and sew the layers together, leaving a 4-in. to 5-in. opening on the bottom edge.

5. Turn the pillow inside out, stuff, then hand-stitch the remaining seam closed. Your pillow is all set for your favorite porch chair!

contributors

The following projects were supplied by contributors for inclusion in Beautiful Burlap:

Chic and Sleek Burlap Tote (p. 12), Double-Stitch Throw Pillows (p. 15), and Place-Setting Pockets (p. 17) by **Lauren Krukowski**. More information on Lauren and her work can be found on her website, laurenkrukowski.com.

Take-Your-Place Placemats (p. 14) by **Lisa Lemieur**. More information on Lisa and her crafts can be found on her website, picklesandcheeseblog.blogspot .com.

Grain Sack Planter Pouch (p. 20) by **Shayna Orrino**. More information on Shayna and her crafts can be found on her website, woodgraincottage.com

Shabby Chic Ruffled Lamp (p. 22) by **Terra Shepard**. More information on Terra and her crafts can be found on her website, mama-says-sew.blogspot.com.

Very Vintage Boutonnieres (p. 26) by **Suzannah Stanley**. More information on Suzannah and her crafts can be found on her website, create-enjoy.com.

Burlap Button Baubles (p. 27) by **Kathleen Kraus**. More information on Kathleen and her products can be found at her Etsy™ shop, Trixie Girl.

Home Sweet Home Address Pillow (p. 29) by **Autumn Speer**. More information on Autumn and her products can be found at her Etsy store, Take Flyte Farm.

resources

ETSY

www.etsy.com

Vintage burlap sacks and other items, crafting supplies

BURLAPFABRIC.COM

www.burlapfabric.com

Burlap bags, table runners, and other finished burlap products

ONLINEFABRICSTORE

www.onlinefabricstore.net

Natural and colored burlap by the yard

FABRIC.COM

www.fabric.com

Printed and metallic burlap

JO-ANN STORES℠

www.joann.com

Fabric, sewing, and crafting supplies

MICHAELS®

www.michaels.com

Burlap fabric ad crafting supplies.

WALMART®

www.walmart.com

Burlap fabric and crafting supplies

MAISON DE STENCILS

www.maisondestencils.com

Stencils

If you like these projects, you'll love these other fun craft booklets.

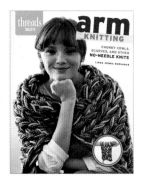

Arm Knitting
Linda Zemba Burhance
EAN: 9781627108867,
8½ × 10⅞, 32 pages,
Product #078045, $9.95 U.S.

Fashionista Arm Knitting
Linda Zemba Burhance,
EAN: 9781627109567,
8½ × 10⅞, 32 pages,
Product # 078050, $9.95 U.S.

Bungee Band Bracelets & More
Vera Vandenbosch,
EAN: 9781627108898,
8½ × 10⅞, 32 pages,
Product # 078048, $9.95 U.S.

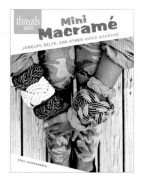

Mini Macrame
Vera Vandenbosch,
EAN: 9781627109574,
8½ × 10⅞, 32 pages,
Product # 078049, $9.95 U.S.

DecoDen Bling
Alice Fisher,
EAN: 9781627108874,
8½ × 10⅞, 32 pages,
Product # 078046, $9.95 U.S.

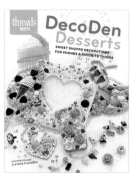

DecoDen Desserts,
Cathie Filian and Steve Piacenza,
EAN: 9781627109703,
8½ × 10⅞, 32 pages,
Product # 078053, $9.95 U.S.

Tie–Dye & Bleach Paint
Charlotte Styles,
EAN: 9781627109895,
8½ × 10⅞, 32 pages,
Product # 078055, $9.95 U.S.

Rubber Band Charm Jewelry
Maggie Marron,
EAN: 9781627108881,
8½ × 10⅞, 32 pages,
Product # 078047, $9.95 U.S.

Super Cute Duct Tape
Jayna Maleri,
EAN: 9781627109901,
8½ × 10⅞, 32 pages,
Product # 078056, $9.95 U.S.

Shop for these and other great craft books and booklets online: www.tauntonstore.com

Simply search by product number or call 800-888-8286, use code MX800126
Call Monday-Friday 9AM – 9PM EST and Saturday 9AM – 5PM EST.
International customers, call 203-702-2204